Richard Pearse

PRIVATE DRIVES

To Conor –
Thanks – Richard Pearse

Selected Poems
1969-2001

RATTAPALLAX PRESS

RATTAPALLAX PRESS
532 La Guardia Place, Suite 353
New York, NY 10012

www.rattapallax.com

Ram Devineni, *Publisher*

Printed in the United States of America

ISBN: 1-892494-38-8
LCCN: 2001116177

Dedication

This book is dedicated to
my daughter, Karina Pearse-LaMalfa,
and to my wife,
Nancy O'Donohue,
for generosity of spirit, both.

I would like to thank the people connected to Rattapallax Press for their support, and particularly to Ram Devineni for publishing this book; and to Richard Levine for friendship and close reading.

CONTENTS

from *Celebrations* (1979)

from *Come Back Vanishing* (1998)

New Poems (1998-2001)

from

Landscape of Skin and Single Rooms

(1969)

TRYING TO SAY IN THE CITY

In the city you can't say what you mean
because you mean everything always
happening at once until
you're evicted, and then who
has time to hear you? It's Saturday night,
and they're all running to punch in before
the constellations crack.

Your last hour on this dark street,
the hour when you and that small white dog
on the leash swallow each other.
He doesn't have a bad life;
he usually says what he means: food, shit, love.

What was it I meant to say?
I need soundtrack music, then I'd know.
I try
barking three notes
that don't know each other
and the mayor steps out
of a junked car, says "You might be
the orchestra our elevators need. Know any
more tunes like that?
Come by my office last year."

LANDSCAPE OF SKIN AND SINGLE ROOMS

They're being careful. Walking
the West Side today not spending
pieces of their faces--a pink rabbit-groove

where that old woman's mouth
was, for this old man's eye
a burrow finely clawed. Because

it's Sunday--who needs
all this heavy wholeness? The energy,
just keeping track! So the pieces

they leave hanging over
the single-room sinks (and
their childhoods drip from Poland's jaw).

When evening leaks the bowls
full, and they come back asking
the wallpaper to hold off tomorrow,

they find the pieces stolen,
along with roses from postcards
and friends' ears from mirrors.

BEGGARS

The accordian's dead
eye swims in
for its smashed
supper, drones you
under the lid
--blood neon and
leg stumps steal
to every hole
your home fell
through, pat your
secret hump for
even a dime,
leave you with
smudged sockets, the
easy blessing. "Any
kind of freakish
feelings are better
than none." By
the time you
know it, you're
glad to die
old. Or run
down Avenue D
where they're all
limping for pity.

ASK ME IN

Moving day. Out of a blizzard
into this old room I drop
my suitcases, photos, spoons,
but nothing gets farther
than my feet in the hallway.
In the drain I hear secrets
clearing their throats, on the way out.
They couldn't stay around
long enough to ask my name.

So I'll assume his, the name
of the previous tenant, dead two weeks.
I'll sit by his mailbox
under the stairs, until
the snow stops, and his smell
of cabbage boiled fifty years
gets used to me, and his other secrets
drift out of their linoleum layers
and ask me in.

from

Fat Chances

(1974)

REPORTING IN

(After Vallejo's "¿Qué me da, que me azoto con la línea . . . ?"

¿What's got into you? You're hanging yourself
by this question mark you knocked over, and all the time
you thought a zero was rolling, following you home.

¿What's got into you? Now you've tied a cactus
around your neck, instead of a diploma.

¿What's got into you, that the human race
is calling it quits after struggling
up to somewhere between your lumbar and thoracic regions,
and turnpikes are taking over from there?

¿What's got into you? You keep weeping
that you've lost your power to weep, and still
your tears refuse to turn you in for the reward.

MARRIAGE

We have our differences.
After I shower she finds feathers in the drain.
I find snail shells in her hat.
Which of us is in the right?

Marriage being as it is, I drop home
through the skylight, she winds out
the hot-water tap. At opposite walls
we take off our shoes
and crawl toward each other
over the warm dragon eggs.

THE RIGHT CONDITIONS

I plan to take only my newest shoes
and cookies I'd been saving for the Crash,
and go at least a hemisphere away,
set up my study with hanging gardens, flares,
all new, and a native girl in back
who can't speak English, to boil the gardenias.

Mornings, the kiss of surf
by the porch, and by ten I'd be
high in a scrim of mist and firs.
Fresh coffee, a brisk run, and settling
down to work, I can discover
dust motes, miracles
of trance under my own fingernails . . .

A Flourishing Mother at Rush Hour

If you're the first, even
at rush hour among
so many, to brush by
her, say with the folded edge
of your evening news,

she'll sprout blood
from every opening.
You'll drown in it.
She'll revive you
with a motherly
mouth, but so badly hurt
herself that she dies.

But not before you
come to--just in time
for her to
forgive you, with
an old smile.

A Futile Mother in the Country

She ran out of the house
throwing stones in all directions--unending
generosity!--and calling to
us, her chldren, as we walked away
down the country road:
"Survive your sons!"
Survive your sons!"
                  And we took it
for a warning, since
her own, her favorite moon
was beginning to shine blackly
through the gaping spaces between beams
in her rotting roof, behind her.

AFTERNOON IN A FAR TOWN

Before the old lady can dust her piano keys,
their crevices begin to fill
with fine jawbones of buffalo.
The shop window at the end of the street
is leaning toward the timberline and
five dusty shoes keep nudging the strings
blowing in from the north clouds.
Now I can see the timid boy I was,
forty years ago, wishing to avoid all voices,
thinking, as long as I fall through the strings,
this is a good afternoon.

Tonight the Widows Are Sailing

Out over Main Street from
their overturned
porches, they
sail tonight, the street
washes gallons of
nuggets in torrents
from the ghost town
mining camps, and over
the bright flood, in
robes scooped out of stars,
their grandfathers dance.

ALL DAY OUT HERE

The endlessness
hell merely promises
is out here: no trees
or shadows to
focus the land, no
valleys to wait
for word from you,
love, did you
ever find my promises,
the ones I left
in the hole in
your smile? They
might have explained
everything, or
almost, and if
not, my God, what
happened to all
the things we said
we'd do together?
They must be
burrowing blind
under six states
of wheat by now,
how will they ever
find you, sleeping
on wheels the way
you always did
when I knew you?

II

Only the land-
line, no trees to
stop it, and this
old lady's bike
rattling up.
            "Here!
Why not you? Take it
and shut up. I
gotta run."

            And
wrapping up the
only road in
her back wheel,
leaving me this
old telegram:
TO AVOID CONFUSION
BE ASSIGNED DEATH-
DAY but the sun
had rubbed out
the rest, not
even a STOP, no
wonder she didn't
have to pick and
choose, with after
all only one man
in sight out here
and the husks
shaking with nowhere
to point but up
at all the sky
with only night's
thumb to fill it.
No wonder it takes
all day out here.

ACCIDENTS ON THE HIGHWAY

You lie down with your sadness,
the weeds poking into your back,
until the scooping and chuffing beside you
proves that highways aren't interested
in running over you;
instead, in heat, they want to run over each other.

And they do, until the countryside is thick
with their long bones.

Lying beside a dead highway
you see how small your sadness is.
You move over and lie on the center stripe.

You are alone with your sadness.
Nothing is going to come along.

You and your sadness
lean closer, touch, causing
a feeble flare, becoming
each other's accident.

OBLIGATIONS TOWARD MY SHOES

Without complaining my shoes have assumed my exact weight.
Without complaining. I grew fat
and pressed them harder. They never squeaked.
I stomped them over dogshit. They took the stink,
not me; over roses, they took the guilt.

Now they're exhausted.
They lie on their cracked sides under the bed.
Slowly they grow. Whatever they brush against turns into night:
first the bed, then the cabin, then the sky.

Finally they relent, allow a chilly dawn. It's time.

I get up and climb the back hill (for once I'm carrying them).
I soak them with gasoline.
I abide by their last requirement: I step into them and
       light the match.

This is better: my smoke isn't weighing down theirs.

In the middle of the sky, the calves that died to make them
are lifting their heads. In welcome? Derision? What?

WHO CAN SAY WHAT THE DEAD MISS MOST?

At twilight down this country road
the hair of the dead grows darkest in the trees,
swims in yellow strands in the long grass.
My car passes the secret lawns,
their owners blue with the mystery of their TVs.
The day's work, fumbled badly,
floats out the car window to the sky.
On the radio the local team is losing
by such a wide margin you can see,
the last of the ninth, how they live
in the shadows of their warmup jackets,
and the final fly hanging
half in shade, and the bullpen bench emptying
slowly into its own purpose above the gravel.
Who can say what the dead miss most?
But with all night and day to go over
their absolute decisions,
the questions of love they won or lost by,
it may well be this hour
they join most easily,
they celebrate with their vague hair.

I Have to Live

The old man is walking through the field.
His suit is a black sack.
His suitcase bangs softly against his leg.
(Inside are relics of me, the ones he tried to trade
       for his future, because he has to live.)

Rain is falling.
It falls within a foot of his bald head, then relents
       and slants off.
Out in the pasture a child is booming a bass drum.

The old man's eyes are closed.
If I call out his name, they will fly open,
       the sockets empty and red.
The rain will beat on his head.

If I call "Messiah!", his mouth will gape and blood
       spurt from the gaps in his teeth.
If I call out my own name and say "Remember me?"
       his suit will rip, his pale chest crack open
       and make a shallow grave for the rain,

the rain that comes closer to his head now,
as I start to open my mouth. I have to live too.

Daddy Bad-News

can stab our cats mid-
squeal and walk
away sleeping, a legend
to us, his dear heirs.
Never takes disasters
for granted, no, only
the remains of them home
to his desk that draws
absolute evening in
over his choicest
autopsies, quilted
and cozy all winter in
the Discipline file.

HOME TOWN   GHOST TOWN

because nobody I know   some old kinsman
keeps howling my ears   full of void
because I need a few ghosts   I found nothing
breathing   on the ash road here

not those dark walls   drifting
not that minister   ticking in his shroud
not that moosehead over the bar   mumbling some lullaby
so this is it   home   it almost
changes so fast and never
answers every time   and I wouldn't mind
returning the favor

that radiant jukebox   do I find its whine
lugubrious   my ass   am I dying as slowly
as these elders stampeding quietly   out onto the freeway
do I care what happens   to my friends wives family if any

because I really need a few ghosts
there's this fat remittance check   I eat
unsalted   because when did I cry last

so this is it   exile   well
I never saw   anything unlike it

ASKING TO LEAVE MYSELF BUT KEEP MY MEMORY

I asked the man behind the counter.
He pointed out to the field

and said "Clear it first."
I started to. Then a thin voice

whispering a hymn
by the far fence.

As I lifted the dead straw, the Victrola
kept on scraping "Bringing in the sheaves."

What I wanted then was a long snowfall.
But the sunlight kept pouring, spreading,

helping the hair of my grandmother grow.
I'll never clear this field.

EARN PITY AND AWE IN SPARE TIME

After all, Garbo and Beethoven are done
to death every day
on the tube, on the air; any wonder then
your family takes you for granted?

Suppose you grew a foam-green beard,
limped home on a comet?
No, even then they'd be blind
to the broken god you are.

Instead, cultivate rarity.
Sit in your dark office after hours.
On some star, a royal robe is beginning
to turn in your direction.

Its advent will perfect your rarity.
You can lean your head on the desk
and dream of its folds opening for you,
its grave guffaw.

FAT CHANCES

He is running to keep from getting fat on women.

Run!--whenever he thinks of all the calories in so much
as their earlobes. Never a nibble at a plump breast--no no,
not so much, only a quick glance, then pound around the track
another hundred laps.

Ah, but all the women in the trees, under the parked cars,
surrounding him, beseeching: Here, touch and taste, all these,
our intricate apertures and syrups . . .

No!--faster faster
until I fly,
gaunt arrow for the eye
of the Denying God!

My flesh be run to sweat,
His tears of joy,
and I be spirited at last
to His home, be His best,
His truest vapor-trail.

THE ADDICTS

Ah you, my favorite chair!
Just when I wanted to fall on you

a comet fell first. Damn!
But I shall show it
manners: "Have a margarita? A lampshade? Mind
if I put on sunglasses?" But it only
rolls around on you--ah you, my favorite chair.

My wife comes home with groceries and
is incandesced; the comet has glanced her way.
She sits beside it murmuring "Me
me you me you me me." Her nails
glow, she is immolated, herself
and the groceries. I predict many nights
of eating out for me,

                              and also many revels
invented to roll
this damn comet hilariously
off you--ah you, my favorite chair!

How to Ward off Burglars

I

I am not real. Quit waving at me.
I am put here every
night, by this bright office window,
at this desk, in this white shirt,
to ward off burglars.
The city is dangerous. Why don't you go home?

II

Put on a red hat.
Bang on your closet
at frequent intervals
to ward off burglars.

Call up some friends.
Throw a party.
Throw sharks
out the window--sometimes
that confuses burglars.

III

Why keep bothering me? Write out your number,
hold it up against the window,
and in another nightmare I might have
asked you out for a drink.
But now there are burglars everywhere,
fitting our darkness better all the time.

WHERE YOU WERE LAST SEEN

It's late, somebody should have been here
to keep these miles from filling
the freezer, even
ten minutes before you walked in.

But when you have to lift
the floor yourself, there's
a note under the wires--
ah, then somebody *was* here, even
if only the burglar.

So the least you can do
in return for the dark is
fade into the wall, your shoulders
taking gray root, your shoes
shuffling off the floor plan
into a movie usher's memory,
where you were last seen.

from

Celebrations

(1979)

DANCING OUR FAMILY DEAD

(variation on a theme by Carlos Drummond de Andrade)

These are the photographs of our family dead. My
grandfather, in goggles and puttees, is climbing out
of his biplane. My great-grandmother waits with her
pies for the baking contest to begin.

We have propped up the photographs in chairs around
the living room, and hung the heavy black clothes on
the wall. Tonight we are having a party. We are laughing
at the earnestness of the bonnets and collars. We are
taking the clothes off the wall and putting them on. We
are dancing, holding the photographs for partners.

As we dance, we laugh harder. The heaviness of their
steady frowns into the future!

We will be dancing our family dead until very late,
time to pack away the clothes and photographs and say
goodnight, and our family dead will reach out once again
to put us to bed. Once again we will close the lid of
the trunk in time.

ASHAMED OF ANY FIRES

These children are laughing are running through the library with torches. The librarian says I am responsible. I never saw them before.

I am being led away, handcuffed. The library is in flames.

Who are these children? Will they visit me in prison? No, they will be flying on their way laughing to Vera Cruz by the time I am sentenced.

Besides, if they were to visit me, even with roses so white there could be no confusing the petals with the flames from their torches, I would be too ashamed to see them.

Even as their steps were to come nearer, my hands would fly up to my face, concealing, burning.

Your Abandoned Child, New Jersey

At Babe Harm's Bar off the turnpike, the weeds are poking through the veterans in back, and the parakeet by the door wants to be a gas pump in the largest station in Wyoming, and never sleep.

You go in there to change a twenty. No more change, no words either, the hubcaps have whirred them away. In return, they've left jowls floating a foot over the bar, and eye sockets covered with fly-screens.

Over each screen, a miniscule flag of New Jersey.

Babe sees the flags and comes over to scorch each one with a rye. Then he counts the zeros that surface around the black fingernails.

Beyond the back marsh is the endless swamp you've crawled from. There, the stranded whale would dip its eyelid one more time before collapsing into factories.

GETTING BACK AT

I called her up to get back at her; she used to like me. I waited for the Hello? she'd give anybody. Then I hung up.

The next time I called she said Stop it, and the next time, You're not funny.

The next time she let the phone ring. It rang and rang as if she'd turned the volume dial all the way off. So I left it ringing and went to sleep. She'd have to turn it back on and answer or she'd be cutting herself off from the world completely.

The next morning it was still ringing. And the next. Finally I went out and got a job. But when I got back, it was still ringing.

Then I decided on a little travel, maybe Madagascar. But I only got as far as the grocery before I had to go back and check. Yep, still ringing.

Then I figured it out. She must have gotten a new phone, probably unlisted, and kept this one ringing just to spite me. And meanwhile *her* life was sailing ahead.

So to get back at her *I* got a new phone, and *mine* was unlisted too. And I had my life--sledding parties, changing jobs with the seasons, kids around the house, the old story. We all just by-passed the open receiver.

Finally I put partitions around the phone and flew off on business to Mantua. But I only got as far as the old high school, where I was kidnapped by coolies and ransomed, then deported back home. Yep, still ringing.

Either I was getting weaker with the years or it was getting stronger--whichever, its ringing knocked down the partitions just as the coroner came in.

And when he asked me to name the greatest satisfaction of my life, I could honestly say it was getting back at her. Just then the ringing stopped. She answered Hello.

I said nothing. She said Hope the man I sent over got there in time.

I said nothing. She said Nice talking to you.

I said nothing. I knew who she was all right, but as long as I kept quiet, she couldn't know me.

THE VISITING DISTINGUISHED, OR DO YOUR OWN WEEPING

Because you are the Visiting Distinguished and because our whole city is celebrating your illustrious *Treatise on Weeping,* I am giving a party in your honor and discussing with you some prominent instances of weeping I myself have observed in men's rooms, offices, airports, etc. My other guests are waiting to join the discussion; let them wait.

But suddenly a giddy coed invades our conversation and says to you "But Sir, don't you think we should just get together, like, and do our own weeping? I mean, I loved your *Treatise,* it was so exhaustive and insightful and all, but wouldn't you like to come with me to the bedroom so we can see how it would be to weep together?"

When he comes back they are both weeping, he blubbering over her--"My baby kidnapped!" and she bewailing him--"My aged daddy in ruins!" My conversation with him is, obviously, shattered. And as soon as everyone else hears them, they all begin to weep over each other--"Your ebbing funds!" "O God the taxes on your angst!" and I find myself weeping over them all--"Alas, waly waly, oi weh!"--and wiping my eyes on my copy of his *Treatise,* which I had hoped he would autograph for me.

A JEALOUS HUSBAND

Tonight my room sails out, burning with the question: is my wife still sleeping with me, or is she only warming up my statue instead?

Just to see, I phoned in a bomb threat to her. I said "Clear it out!" and God did she! Pajamas, antlers, moose-flares, the chandelier--they came tearing-ass down the stairs, with all the bitchiness of having to leave a room too fast.

But when the stampede passed, she wasn't there--oh no, not her! So I knocked on the door, but the door ran out too, leaving me with nothing but the snow from my own telephone. She couldn't even bother to leave me a decent memo--and that's what made me give her up, let the sky in through my eyes, and this such a huge night to fly up into!

WHAT HAPPENS TO FATHERS AND CHILDREN

More children keep being born.

Because at night the fathers go off alone on long drives,
anywhere. They stop suddenly and walk into the woods.
They complain to their future:

"I need you. The children I have are all ungrateful. They
never come to see the abandoned bridge where my name is
nailed. They turn their sleep away from mine. I should
have cancelled them all!

"So I want you to come back to the house with me. Every
time we sit together, I'll find myself younger, I'll lose
one more child. Finally I'll be free of them completely.
I'll have only you, you'll take care of me. Please come!

"Or else I'll have to try again, make another child with
only the same old equipment: night, whiskey, and my wife."

It doesn't work. They walk back to their cars alone.

More children keep leaving.

Because, alone in the house, the children climb up to
the attic. They complain to their past:

"Quit blocking the sky. I'm leaving with it because it
reminds me of me, not you. And I hate you because you
remind me of you, not me. Get out of the way!"

They they put on antique clothes for disguises, sell

the house, change their names, run up to the roof, try
to fly off. They fall and start crawling. Always away.

More fathers keep traveling.

Because, by the time the fathers get back to the house,
it's morning and the moving men are just carrying off
the last picture of them, the last chair.

More fathers keep wanting to die.

Because now they have to drive off with the daylight
in front of them. Worse than being alone.

The Hiding Wife

The man would come home from work to look for the wife.

It was the wife's custom to hide parts of herself all
through the kitchen. Sometimes a nose in one niche of the
spice rack, then a nipple in another. In summer, some
parts would often be secreted in the ice-tray; in winter,
in the muffin-tin.

Only after the man had found the parts could he know that
he was really in the home and not in a strange home, with
the wife and not with a strange wife, with the man himself
and not with a stranger.

But one day the man couldn't find the wife. No parts in
the kitchen--an insurrection? No parts in the bedroom--a
rival man? No parts in the bathroom-livingroom-den--a rival
home?

The man forgot the man's name and started saying Joe.
Another drink Joe? Sure. The man forgot the wife's name.
Remember Marge Jack? Sure. Remember the way she used to
butter the Betty bread with the Esther knife Jim? Right.
And make that another drink.

Finally the man staggered out of the home because it was
time to go to work. He patted the door. Bye-bye 2842 Maple
Lane. Since that wasn't the home's name, the door closed
after him. The man won't be back, the man thought.

The home knew that. The wife knew. The wife had hidden
so well that she had entwined with the home, the wife
spreading through the pipes, the home spreading through
the veins. The transfiguration, with its roof of blonde hair,
began to darken the neighborhood.

50

CALLING HOME FROM NOWHERE

Night now and nothing for it but to call home. Once a
year this night, the night of my conception, falls on my
head and there's nothing for it.

But shouldn't I at least try an assumed name? No sense
giving myself away at the start. And who should I be?
Who do they admire at home? Anybody alive?

No, and I can't imitate the dead. But then shouldn't I
promise them a gift? But what gift could possibly explain
why I waited here so long, with nothing to show for it?

All I have is their future, all I can do is wrap it up, get it
over with. So I dial, I wait, my breath falls into the black
holes of the receiver, under the busy signal. Somebody
got their first. Somebody else is going to have to be
conceived tonight.

LAZY JOYS AND BLUES

The man in my hallway mirror is a better man than
I'll ever be. I lose laundry, he finds clients. I forget
appointments, he remembers invitations that haven't
been extended yet.

I leave him problems to solve, such as estimating
my taxes after provisional reincarnation, and in the
morning his answers are tucked in the pocket of our
blue shirt, always fresher-looking on him. They're
written backwards of course, but *he* can read them.

(Always about 28, perfect shape, good tan. Always
lives in season.)

It seems I may be dismissed from my position. It
is imperative that he emerge from the mirror to make
any necessary reparations for me. *Note:* must keep the
mirror clean to facilitate his emergence.

(Always that capable smile. Any moment now he'll come.)

But the man in my *bathroom* mirror? Don't ask. With
his wrinkles sagging into a map of perpetual defeat,
he's going to be the death of me.

WAKING TO THESE STATES

Waking to these states my future in sky blue. Up
from the operating table. Smells of ice. My teachers
are here. Having taught me glass all these years,
they've gone behind their own glass, to watch how the
surgery went.

Waking to my new room, all the coat-pegs empty, a
new peg sprouting up every few feet, coast to coast.
Between the pegs small flames keep starting.

Waking to my new job to pay the medical bills: I
count the flames, report how frequently they turn to
the color of bone and point downward.

Waking to these states waking to these states saying
the operation was a success.

THE SMILE OF A CONFIDENT MAN

The confident man may be discerned by his manner of entering an elevator: neither too quickly, just after the door opens, nor too slowly, just before it closes. And with the slight smile of a psychiatrist entering a room half-full of his patients. Moves all the way to the side, in consideration of the claustrophobia or social pathologies of others.

The smile stays. The elevator descends. It is the end of the work day, but the suit is still neat, and a martini is waiting around the corner, in a small lounge by the Plaza.

The confident man does not fidget or scratch or say "Whew!" as the others inside do, to remind themselves that they are still there. Rather, he glances at a smudge that used to be graffitti. The smile stays; if anything, it grows.

The elevator stops at the twelfth floor. No one is there. The others groan at this delay and shuffle forward, causing the door to catch before it can close. But the smile stays.

It stops at the tenth floor. Four people edge in. It stops at the ninth floor: three more, and now it is packed. Crushed between a paunch and a corsage, the suit is wrinkling a bit. But the smile stays, in acknowledgement of the discomfort of others.

A whine, a scrape. Then a stop. Between the eighth and seventh floors. They are trapped: one soft shuddering sound from a woman, a series of threats against the city from a man. The smile grows, tilting up at the edges, in acknowledgement of the terrors of others.

The fan ticks twice and goes off. They are sweating, gasping but afraid to breathe. Then the light dims and dies. Curses, a moan, somebody pummeling the door. The suit is a map of wrinkles. The smile spreads.

The smile opens, begins to gleam in the dark. The others are gradually dissolving, melting like wax into its cave. One by one, slowly, they are sliding into the smile, which is growing to accommodate them. It is filling the elevator. Finally the confident man himself is going: the smooth forehead slides downward into it, the neck and shoulders curl and slope upward like smoke. Then the entire body, including the ruined suit.

No movement. Nothing but the smile. Soon the workmen will break open the door and shine their flashlights inside, and the smile's gleam will disappear. But the smile will still be there. It will spread out to the lobby, along 59th Street, through the Park and the entire midtown area, so great is its confidence.

EARNING A NAME

He's crazy, he meets you at every corner, no matter
how early and your pockets pink with titles, or late
and the business of dead bats in your briefcase, and
he always says "How about a game?"

But it's too easy--to win, you do what you're doing,
keep your head up, one foot at a time finding your weight
until you're across. It's everybody's habit!--and you
tell him so and he says "Sure, but who knows? Sometime
you might get bored, always the same two feet. Maybe
you'll want a change--fall down and let the sirens do
the work, or maybe fly and watch the crowd collect."

Over and over you try to tell him you cross these
streets for better reasons. A family, a name, foreign,
indecipherable, waiting to be earned. But already
his question's jumped down to the next corner.

THE DILATING THEATER

A wife said to her husband "I'm going crazy!"

He answered "Really? Well of course it's your own business, but let me tell you if you do, so will I, who have more cause, and I'll be a hell of a lot quicker about it, and then we'll see who has to take care of whose bedpan!"

She said "You competitor! Just for that I've already gone crazy and the documents were signed long ago!"

He said "Oh? We'll just see whose documents are dated earlier!"

They saw each other often after that, going down the staircases on the opposite walls of their tower, and sometimes coming back up.

WHAT ARE FATHERS FOR?

Your son is lost and what are fathers for? Quick--rush into the forest to find him.

(Somewhere in the desert he's lurching around looking for the huge pinball machine.)

Could you find him in the hollow center of a dead tree? Quick, before the tree splinters and he's gone again!

(The pinball machine that shoots red filaments up to the desert sun. One more hit and he could climb the filaments.)

Could you find him if you knock on enough trees and listen for the echo? Quick, before it starts to get dark!

WOMAN, CELLO, CHILD

In the woods the woman is playing the cello, practising
for her recital in a deeper part of the woods.

The small child comes up and hugs her as she plays. The
music begins to burrow beneath the roots of trees.

The child starts slapping at the strings of the cello.
The music begins to skim up into the tops of trees.

The woman draws the bow across the child. The music
begins to fan out through the woods, past the freeway,
into the suburbs.

Now the child is crying. Strikes the woman. The music
rushes into the center of town, and the buildings crack,
topple down over the streets with their own music, to bring
everyone to the particularly musical dying everyone wants.

DEAR MOTHER,

I would have remembered your birthday, but the sun
celebrates its own by poking holes in my ceiling, day
after day. Then the moon retaliates by filling them
with small moons. What an egotist the sun is. And what
a distraction the moon. At twilight, though, it's a
problem of statues toppling through my door. How is it
with you? Would you please leave your childhood ribbons,
anything intimate, by the dark stream that leads to my
door? It can remember better than I. I'd like to add
more news, but the wind is blowing my hand away to its
mother the storm. Love,

STARTING THE WORKDAY RIGHT

"No no no! How many times do I have to tell you--
build the body first, then its coffin, or it won't fit!

"Even if it's your own Dad, Dad?"

"*Especially* then. Or it'll get in your way the whole
workday!"

A Hope for My Child, Not Yet Born

Driving cross-country. Beside me, my mother talking
baby-talk. My father in back, dead.

My father driving deaf, crashing into the factories
he built. Me beside him afraid to ask why. My mother
in back dead and getting ready to talk baby-talk.

My mother driving blind, crashing into the churches
she bought. My father beside her afraid to ask why. Me
in back, crying at finding myself still locked in this
car after death.

All three of us in back, dead. Me trying to argue
but finding myself talking baby-talk, my words beating
against the doors. The car heading for my child.

My child picking up the toy car, flipping it up in
the air, laughs.

Remembering a Friend

Friend, there was a memory, really a private eye,
going around with his hat low, asking questions.

About you. He wanted to shadow you, here under
these abandoned rafters.

"Especially here. Because a shadow needs shade."

So he lay there bleeding from the bullets he gamely
kept shooting into himself, over and over, in the back of
the barn that was being torn down.

THE BARBER SHOP OF THE DEAD

You've left the hot, bright highway for this shade
you deepen into.

All afternoon you try to catch their attention. They
never look up, cutting the thin hair meticulously,
scissors twittering.

On the radio, the pitcher is holding the ball, staring.
The old headlines are backwards; you have to hold them up
to the dark mirror.

It's all right. Because your car is just outside and you
can feel your keys. Because at home and at your office
the phones are going to ring. And because your hair keeps
on growing. That's why you sit here, as the summer
spreads out over you.

WHO FELL AWAY FIRST?

It was my child who fell away out the door.

The solution? I asked the door, which is always full of
its boundaries and decrees.

"The solution here is that you should have kept me closed."

I've always disliked the door. "Thank you very much. But I
need a solution for the future."

"The solution there is that you must fall away also. Then
nobody can blame you for forgetting who fell away first."

"Thank you very much. But my own memory--"

"Stop arguing" it said and slammed shut, pushing me out.
So I fell away and, forgetful of gravity, up. Not to be a dead
star, oh no, not so much, but only to join all the spaces between.

THE RECOLLECTION-HOLE

The middle-aged man decides to cut a hole in his
breakfast table, to stick his finger in and so carry
around the table, the recollection of his breakfast.

But never a hole in his lunch nor his supper table,
he cautions himself. Moderation!

When next breakfast time comes, the hole has grown--
was he immoderate in his carrying?--so that his knife
and fork and bacon and toast are all falling through it,
the yolk of his egg bending So-Long. He reaches after
them, but not too fast, he cautions himself. Always
moderation!

But suddenly hunger, the immoderate lust for breakfast-
recollection, seizes him and throws his hands down the
hole, then his elbows-shoulders-head--too fast!--down past
his breakfast-recollection down past his last-night's-sleep-
recollection down past his youth-recollection down past his
life-even-before-birth-recollection. O the sorrow of insufficient
moderation! says somebody's recollection of the middle-aged
man before it too begins to pour down the hole, bending
So-long.

from

Come Back Vanishing

(1998)

DOOM & ME

Hello there, Ultimate Doom, how are things?
        All these years you've been doing my job for me,
isn't it time you relaxed? Here,
        have some tea, I forget
how you take it, take it my way,
        milk & honey. Here,
here's the cup for your cloudy hands.

I've been trying off & on to keep the books
        on us, our empires, those world wars...
easy to get behind, though. You know how it is,
        so many things to notice every day
on this one little block of newsstands & delis.

Plus I've got my hobbies. I took up the kazoo,
        did I tell you?--here, let me hum
something for you--no no, don't go yet!
        Why so touchy over a little light music?
Have another cup, stay--you almost never come
        around these days, let me at least say thanks--
where would I be without you?

THE DISCREET GUEST

breaks into your house
        expertly, never wakes you, repairs the lock

goes up to your study
        improves your work, your own handwriting but neater

always exits before you wake
        has your coffee brewed and warming

leaves a brief note
        thanking you for your hospitality

praising your charm
        and wit, your wife's intelligence, beauty, grace

invites you over
        signs his nickname, all lower case letters

You tear up the note
        rage through your rooms cursing him

In every corner
        you see your obsolete papers, dirty clothes, dust

You stop your wife
        from packing up and leaving you for him

only by reminding her
        once more of the other guest, even more discreet

waiting for you alone
      every night in your driveway, in her silver convertible

the moon washing over her skin
      breeze stirring the folds of her luminous dress

MISTAKES OF WAKING URBAN

Difficult, this quick
        disgorging of your fingers *just*
in time to grab the sun
        before it breaks
your window--right, all apologies due
        the just-eclipsed skyline, but please,
who needs another wrecking ball?

And don't dream
        biting off the pythons
wrapped around your eyes is easy either.
        By now you're late--
the International Pro-Defenestration Conference
        has begun, and you never
planned your keynote speech?

Planned? Termites could have planned
        this rotting sky; just unravel their antennae
and ease all the way out
        onto the street, where the wind tunnels
shrug. There's a quick smoke but no time,
        a corner to turn, the heft
of this cell phone to celebrate, and how
        the buildings, their shuffling altitudes,
lose your friends' voices. Think: for this
        and more, more than you can hold,
you gave up your best bits of colored glass!

And as the office morning frays,
        you're gradually consumed by desire
for the lost breast, last sighted
        drifting underneath some colleague's blouse.
(Whose? Does it commute downtown?)

Honestly, all you ever wanted from this town
   is the object of that board game
you'll play tonight at Jay's off Gramercy:
   "To commit as many mortal sins
as possible, and still die in a state of grace."

YOU CAN TOO

Take for instance   my chosen career
of pleasing everyone   by riding in funeral processions
beside the corpse   both of us displayed
high on mounds of roses   the sunlight blaring like brass

The crowds of mourners   all want me out
so they can grieve   undistractedly
and I try to placate them   I offer to fall from the hearse
they say Go ahead!   but of course there are laws
so instead they curse me   for his sake   their dear departed's

And as we proceed to the cemetary   rain vague as tears
they're engrossed with me   they forget his faults
truly I'm the best friend   of all concerned

(What if God at the Gates asks of us   Why
did you all love yourselves so little?)   I am paid
generously in advance   by the family and friends
those passionate evasives   nominal liberators
who all want only   to be in the right   after all

THE LADY OF THE WASTES

O Lord what made me want
to buy up this slum,
put my name in red lights on the fire escapes,
and send out photos on Christmas cards:
"Hi Friends--wish you lived here!"

Like a teeth sandwich before breakfast,
this decision.

So thank God I heard of you, friend
of a friend, Lady of the Wastes--you
took all the tenements
off my hands, burned them down
for your birthday candles, willingly shared
the insurance money:
generous enough so now I could buy
a lean-to in the country,
a couple of dead dogs,
and live off their maggots, humble at last.

Friend of a friend, wife
of all bachelors, to me you were more
than a talk-show hostess at dawn; to you
my gratitude runs in the bad blood between us
like wooden legs.

WHEN YOU DIE IN NEW YORK

you're already running late
and there's no office cheap enough
to rent for your body's loosening decay.

When you die in New York
you find yourself on avenues blown empty of everyone
including you, or you wander over
to your family's door, your collar up
though you don't feel the sleet
ruining their weekend plans.

When you die in New York
your breath and hands won't stay clean
for your scheduled interviews
with the homeless, in their dreams
as they turn and turn on their cardboard pallets.

When you die in New York
you inherit your empire at last:
the exorbitant slum
lodged in the eye of that commuter,
causing him tears
as he spurts to catch the late train home.

LONG DARK ENTANGLEMENTS

I believed her long dark hair
flaring over the dirt road,
hair that long & dark
could shut out neon
once she climbed on top, & all sanity too.
Fine. Turn the nightmares loose--
we could flay them alive with that hair.

High over the Drive, we flicked
our ashes at the morning rushers. Me,
I was hooked on her hair
& living off my savings, why not.

& I did give her some first-rate
mementos, hieroglyphs, had her head
carved onto onyx. No half-steps. Late,
when I believed she was asleep,
I'd breathe it in, that long dark hair.

Once I saw her walking
away, I followed. Gone.
Where I am now, eye contact
is discouraged.

Never a good idea
taking on a stray angel, trying
to fly on her hair.

ROMANCE LANGUAGE LESSON

Hello, am I Ricardo? This is the subway, is it not? Are you
beautiful? Or am I pathologically deluded? Can you imagine my
nerves upon seeing you? If this is Thursday, am I well on my way
uptown to see my dentist? Or if Friday, am I hosting the senator
this evening and journeying downtown to gather flowers for him?
What are your favorite flowers? Colors? Jewels?

You are undoubtedly possessed of a sublime and variegated life
history, true? Too painful to discuss easily, as is mine also?

Are we now out on the ocean? Are we now on our way to a new life
together, perhaps to Barcelona? To Minsk? Mogadishu? Is this a lucky
break for me?

How do you like this picture of my grocer? Of my aforementioned
dentist? Would you enjoy meeting my wife and three sons? Do you see
how open I am being with you? Are we soon to find ourselves ensconced
in your Upper East Side *pied-à-terre?*

Offhand, do you believe it possible to construct an all-time all-
star Notre Dame football team? In one conversation only? Have you a
favorite Callas aria? What is your best weather?

Am I overjoyed? Are we aloft yet? Am I near my stop?

May I see you again please? Is there anything you wish to tell me?
Some recent achievement or indiscretion perhaps? Or some homage to
your war-hero husband and to his illustrious family and of course to
your five children, as well as to your many other relatives, too
numerous to mention and yet each one deserving of special praise?
Do you prefer to speak from notes?

Are you near your stop? What are your dreams? In them do you
fear exams in school? In them are you ever nude? Are others? How
nearly nude in public do you normally become? Am I overstepping
myself? Would you prefer to hear how nearly nude I have often
made myself, on occasions when public propriety was *de rigueur?*

Are our stops the same, or is that too much to hope? Would you
consider marrying me, once the legal paperwork of my domestic
situation is resolved, a matter of weeks at the most? Or do you
believe that marriage is an obsolete institution? What are your
views on contraception? Do you prefer extended engagements, or
sudden elopements with ladders, horses, gunshots?

What is your name? Your age, height, weight, nationality? Do
you speak English? Spanish? Urdu? Or perhaps some lovely Slavic
tongue? Is your tongue beautiful? Are your legs? Your cleavage
in this light? Would you care to say anything at all concerning
your vulva?

Is your love commensurate to mine? Have you cash for an extra
fare? Shall we continue on this train past your stop, past mine,
past all possible stops so long as this delirium shall endure, in
other words forever? Oh you have mesmerized me so--am I Ricardo?

WOMEN

You go out for a walk
on the corner a shabby old woman has fallen down
you help her up oof what an odor
thank you would you like a job she says
I'm really quite wealthy albeit eccentric in dress & habits
so you sit behind your gleaming new desk
you open some mail you phone home
your wife crying tells you she just miscarried
you start crying too
your reflection there in the polished desk
you stand up to go to her
your secretary comes in with more mail
you sit back down
seeing you in grief she sits on your lap
she tickles you & you laugh
you two go out for lunch you touch her under the table
after dessert you lean back and recite--

> Boon to the pregnant Hottentots, I move
> From factory to chapel, blessing all
> The succubi, the socialites, the Wool-
> Worth ladies, and those tipsy-dead for love.

poetry isn't my thing she says but you have a nice voice
she goes back to the office
you go out for a walk
a woman window-shopping catches your eye
familiar yes
she's your childhood sweetheart your first crush
she notices you following her & points you out to a cop
so you head for home
on the way you remember flowers for your wife
at home on the fridge a note from her
she's left you & gone off with her gynecologist

a woman who understands women she says
you start crying
your reflection there in the kitchen window
the phone rings it's your mother
how could you have forgotten my birthday again she says
you decide to take her the flowers
on the corner a woman in a bright tight dress eyes you
hey wanna go out & do stuff
you hand her the flowers & recite--

       Sweet recreant lasses, who for their misery rove
       Beyond the hotsy-totsy to fulfill
       The all-at-once-alas attainable--
       Snickers abroad their one affianced grove.

she says okay that's it you're under arrest
she's an undercover cop
tipped off by your childhood sweetheart you guess
from jail you phone your lawyer
it's entrapment she says
don't worry the charge won't stick
freed on bail you get back your flowers
maybe in time to visit your mother before her nap
on the way you pass a hospital
at the second floor window a nurse is washing a baby
it slips all soapy out of her hands out the window
it falls into the crook of your arm among the flowers
a pink baby girl
your mother is delighted with the flowers
but puzzled that your wife has delivered a baby so early
she says such a healthy baby beautiful but please explain
you tell her you have to get back to the office
she says oh so you have a new job why didn't you tell me
you tell her you've been busy
you say would you mind taking care of this baby for me
she says your wife is an unfit mother I always knew it
but all right sure I'm a sucker I'll raise her up

I'll teach her to keep me informed of her doings
to never be too busy for me
you get back to the office just before quitting time
you sit down at your desk & open your mail
the old woman comes in
you call this an honest day's work she says
you jailbird you're fired
innocent til proven your secretary says
I'll stand by him
so the two of you go for a walk
at the nearest bar you invite her in
thanks but my husband and kids need me she says
alone at the bar you drink like no tomorrow
the woman on the corner stool says rough day I bet
says I'm doing my doctorate on tavern behavior
you ask her to have a drink with you
she says can't drink allergic reaction
but come on back to my place
on her sofa you kiss
she makes herb tea & offers parsley sandwiches
you kiss & caress some more
then you come before she can get her blouse off
tired you lie back on the sofa & recite--

> Alas? At last--for those salt ovaries
> My pilgrimmages live. Not blood alone
> Leads me my blowtorch, humble and awry,
> These mackeral portals lowly to outgroan;
> Nor shall yet ever suffer slaughter's ease,
> But I with maudlin timbrel wash away.

The images are revealing she says
especially that blowtorch on line three
you explain there are lines before these
this is a continuation
okay she says but I still wonder about your obsessions
so you decide to go out for a walk

no matter how tired & the moon down
never too late for a walk

Do-Si-Do

What can I do? I love you,
and you love Carlos, who loves his factories,
which love only their raw materials. Meanwhile,
Sergei loves his one phone call with you
but can't leave his mother, who complains of dizziness.

On the other hand, Myeesha loves a photo of Colin
taken years ago, in a dim light, whereas
Colin loves the romors of Abdul
being bi, and the fact of Lars being gay, although
that fact did not keep Lars' lover, Mario, from suicide.

(Note: this is the same Abdul
who, after divorcing Claudette for adultery,
has sworn to mutilate any man who comes near you.)

And as evening falls on all our quandaries,
where is the smoke from your chimney drifting,
toward what new romance, once I've killed Carlos,
and what chance has my love against the coming nights?

MAIL ORDER

Your new silk suit has arrived,
as splendid as in the catalogue picture,
but so huge it fills the house.

And so expensive! How to send it back
when the company has been merged
into a larger one, with a new name and foreign rules?

Well anyway, room in the pants
for your whole family, and the dogs,
with your furniture hauled in to fill out the waist.

But no walking around,
no movement possible at all
once you've got the neighbors all stuffed into the jacket.

Wait--now you need to rent a truck
where the head would be, exhaust fumes for a scarf.
Now bribe some strangers to hang from the sleeves for hands.

Absolutely stifling
inside all this elegant black silk,
but just keep holding your breath:

any minute now
he's coming, the photographer you commisioned
from the catalogue. He said he was guaranteed.

THE FERRYMAN AND I

I got to his boat just in time
but couldn't find the coin, nothing
smaller in my shroud
than a check for my life savings.

He took it. Professional,
his one-way shades glossy, he poled me across,
then beached the boat and, since I'd paid so much,
insisted on showing me around:

midnight parades of pink spider legs, expensive
fandangoes of blonde convertibles
and a spot for me
on the Float of Mermaids.

Soon enough I got accustomed
to the constant smiling and waving, and found
the necessary balance between charming
the girlies and ghoulies to get by,

yes I did: promoted to Parade Leader
First-Class; but then, professional,
he tapped my shoulder, said
I'd paid so much

he insisted on ferrying me back
round-trip to my native land, perpetual
potential, back to all
the excuses still waiting to die.

RETIREE

My license has lapsed
& I'm turning in
at the Foothills Motel
with my suitcase, gin &
the blonde cheerleader
on 88 channels. I have
no plans further
than her long braids
whipping my belly hairs.

I'm the last swamp in Florida,
the one that didn't sell.
I'm the fat tabby frozen
in the headlights or
your roadside attraction--
Quacky-Wacky Duck Vaudeville
closed down. I'm out
of any promises that held
me firm, held the firm to me.

Maybe my father, the silent
success, wanted grandchildren
skipping around his van,
at least til he pulled out
in the morning, or maybe
the worst--he only wanted
me to succeed, succeed him
by being happy wherever
I managed to lose myself.

Some Alternatives to the Crash
That Killed Sigrid

You drive out on the long flat road
you cross the center line to pass the hay truck
and an old man sky-blue ushers you into a cloud
its caves are folds of light
he invites you to explore
safely safely   no
the sunset would dye everything red

You cross the center line
and turn under the stone arch into an old tavern
whose burghers have been waiting centuries
for your bumper to crack open their barrels
joyfully joyfully   no   it would spill
bleed out onto the cobblestones
the strong red wine

You cross the center line
and see the fire truck head-on and
panicking you flail and hit the reverse gear and
you're plummeted backwards yes now you are starting this drive
now you're buying this car now trying your new tricycle
finally you swim in the womb securely   no
its walls would darken red too soon before birth

You cross the center line
and the truck turns left and your car eases onto its hayload
like a head onto a pillow
the hay willing to hold you
while it dreams of the long fields it came from
peacefully   no   it thrashes in its sleep with the nightmare
its family over at the next farm has caught fire

You cross the center line
but I manage to flag you down
and you climb out your stockings flashing and
on the wrong side of the road we dance slowly to your car radio
my fingers sliding for your breast
stirringly yes where it turns pink at the tip
no   I don't reach down to where your menstrual blood is flowing

You cross the center line
the church doors swing wide
the red-robed priest welcomes you inside
for pentecost time of the tongues of fire
the candle flames climb toward the vault
this is sanctuary you are safe in prayer
no   you do not believe   not any of it

No   no   your car is not red
but the deep green of grass after rain
your smashing dress is not red but the pale blue
of your veins carrying the blood securely
in your hands turning the wheel as you remember
you left behind a letter that must be mailed
oh shit you say softly and then

turn
back
off
the
long
flat
road

ALONZO'S CRIB DEATH

Well, old retrograder, you've paid a steep price
for this vertiginous distance from the plains.

The crone of the mountain pass, her rope bridge
prohibitive--ask *her* for help?--Ha:

might as well try to leap the chasm, manic how
her giggle rises. No, no way out;

reach in your pack and hand over your newborn,
potentially a great wide receiver, if only

the ground would flatten out . . . . Well forget it--
his scream and clatter lost way down the gorge

where she dropped him. Space
under greater space. Still and all,

still and all, this arena of distance mollifies her
but took Alonzo's breath away.

First Day

Tired of the hours and the jokes
at the Stateline Car Wash,
you head off to college. First day,

you sign up for Introduction to Psychology
and wind up in Advanced Sanskrit--the registrar's error,
but maybe connections here

you could pursue--glossolalia, tantric asides,
and the beautiful Hindu teacher, ruby in her navel,
who takes you aside for a conference,

since you're the only one
unqualified, and she wonders about you,
politely. But you join in the exercises:

chanting conjugations of breath.
Toward evening, the class retires
to one huge bed, and she asks you to lecture

on psychology. Is this like vespers
back home? You clear your throat,
wonder where to begin,

but the whole class has fallen asleep,
exhausted by the possibilities of tongues.
As her apology for them,

her ruby glowing a deeper red, and
muttering in the mother tongue you'll never master,
she starts to kiss you for a long time.

A HUSBAND'S OTHERWISE LIFE

Sorry honey, here
I almost stepped on your lame foot.

Did I really lose your life savings
while you were out

waitressing double shifts? Awful--
wish I knew what happened

to that $30,000 you'd put away
for your well-deserved leg operation--or

$300,000? Sorry. Thought
I'd spent it on getting the photos framed

of you & the kids. & really
27 years since we made love? Oh boy.

& to ignore your hot meals
& neatly folded laundry,

immaculate housekeeping--what was I thinking?
Well, & I can't account for the women's numbers,

the racing forms, the dope
you found under the bed--but if mine,

I guess the true meaning of dissipation,
nothing out of something, was me

for sure, but nothing looks familiar--
sorry I can't help you or your therapist,

but I swear I've changed,
so if you'll take me back

we can start anew
without the burden of what

to spend your savings on.
& anyway, I love your limp.

YOUR FORTUNE

Open your right hand. Yes I see
a catastrophe--no, many--
will relieve your morning hours.

But you won't be the only one
crazed by the day-stars' skywriting, to lose
your bearings, your office keys:

the rest of the staff will already
be lurching around the building,
banging on doors. Finally

they all straggle off, and where
each one falls exhausted, a new branch office sprouts.
They want you in Moose Jaw. Refuse to transfer

and be fired. But don't go home for lunch.
Much as you cherish
the memory of your mother's soup,

your wife will have left, drifted next door
to replace the wife there
who drifted one house down, and so on

around the block. Her replacement
at your kitchen table
is Estonian, thin, beautiful

but growls at your approach.
Don't go home. Instead,
walk to the train tracks and old sheds

where the suburbs end. There set out--
but I see your lifeline
has broken. Open

your left hand. Empty.
Yes I see
you're out of money too. Goodbye.

THE PATIENT IS ABOUT TO BE RELEASED

(after Vallejo's "Los desgraciados")

Doctor, the day is coming, ice
in my spine, can't find my head
under the pillow--quick, one more roll
on my neck, then walk a straight line.
The day is coming--quick, on with my skin.

The day is coming--oh hold tight
to stomach & scrotum. Meditate
until you mean: Godawful
when hard times fall
& I fall through all floors.

I have to breathe!--but you,
you tell yourself not to worry,
your independent means can bypass funerals,
& anyway, I'll be all mended tomorrow.
--No. But must remember to believe
without you, in clouds and teeth, count my belongings, keep
the list coiled up my ass. The day
is coming--quick, on with my echoes.

The day is coming, you'll pass my bed,
you've opened a quaint peephole in my skull
& then kicked in the glass . . .
I'm shaking--it's the far reaches of my scalp
& the alliances of my hunger,
but you, you're still snoring with your eyes open!
An empire could be sliding away,
& my God--with all these couples, dyads, duos, pairs--
how singular these walls make me!
The day is coming--quick, on with my selective oblivions.
The day is coming, you keep telling me

through every microphone you yawn. & here I go--
right-hand dizzy spells, left-hand shivers,
& all the terror-jumps between. God help me
if I'm caught, poor as I am,
in the midst of your money. Must remember: stir
very carefully my sweat,
so your air conditioning melts in, you beige diagram.

The day is coming, with canals, conflagrations--
all flags flying. It's hounding my fatigue.
Because my pride's allegedly incorporated,
the janitors here ready their chainsaws, teeth on a leash.
Doctor, I'm trying to warn you: on waking
nobody's not alone, not even you.
The day is coming--quick, on with my orbits.

The day is here--now I must
double my breathing, double again
my affable malice
& hide from context, contagion, control;
because I, being by my own testimony
temporary, dreamed last night,
& will dream again tonight,
that I'm dying from everything,
living on nothing,
& both of them are me.

Bed and Breakfast

Late ailing, I rented a room
in this large old house, shabby but warm,
up the hill at the north end of town,
first floor in front, with a window

so I could sit up in bed
early afternoons and look out at the used snow,
the street curving down and away,
and hear on the stairs

the comings and goings
of the men I'd killed
just by drifting along another road,
those earlier versions of myself:

the drawn serious schoolteacher
who didn't leave his wife and child
(they stay there with him still, thin and nervous,
they don't come down for breakfast),

the messianic preacher who lived alone,
lived by his bibles and notebooks,
waiting for them to open of themselves, reveal
the bridge to God exclusively his own,

the mama's boy who never left home,
never imagined a better friend than her
nor a better entertainer, lover, provider
of more than he could wish for.

Friday afternoons we'd get together
in the living room, set up a table on the worn rug,
play a little blackjack for small stakes.
I didn't have a thing to say

except *aah shit* when the wrong card
slid me over the limit,
and *ooh yeah* when the ace of spades turned up
greasy and lustrous under my thumb.

DO YOU HAVE THIS DISEASE?

Do you laugh suddenly, uncontrollably?
Weep inexplicably?
Have trouble sleeping or waking, moving or standing still?

Do you find yourself a slave of moods
that keep breezing in, taking over your home?
Or of inappropriate ideas (invent a parachute for parakeets?)
Do your dustballs seem incomprehensible? Do your children?

Do you feel the sudden need to urinate on ambassadors?
Do you rub against monuments of heroes until you come?
Do you walk the streets late, demanding a falconry instructor?

Have you married a young adventurous woman only to find her,
after the birth of your eighth child, sinking into despondency
and a dependence upon mail-order catalogues?

Conversely, have you devoted a solitary life to the Salvation Army,
only to discover that your pension has been embezzled away
by the very commander to whom you served your special coffee
piping-hot every morning for 37 years, leaving you with nothing
but this note from him, saying "Sorry!" and enclosing a snapshot
of himself on the beach at Cancun, with a bronzed and bikinied
lovely? Have you stared at the snapshot, turning it this way
and that to catch the gloss, there in your two-room flat over
the auto repair shop, while harboring negative thoughts?

When you go to the shopping mall, do you neglect to wear comfortable
yet firmly supportive shoes? Do you frequently forget who you
are, a failed consumer with insufficient funds? Do you find
yourself staring at the rows and rows of goods, waiting for them
to take you? Waiting for God to give them to you? Waiting for
a night that will never end?

100

DARK'S LAST CASE

So I got back late, my head banging the breeze,
on-off EAT sign drilling the old migraine, when I saw
the note under my door--"Got tired of running.
You want me, I'm down the hall."

I was new on the case, but the angel's handwriting
checked. Handy. Now if he'd just waited
til banker's hours in the morning . . . a joke, brother.
No hours, not in this business. So I eased off
the safety, put on the silencer, checked my shine & shave.

The blood was spreading out from under his door
before I could open it. His robe & wings
were soaked. A note--"I confess. The plans
for joy are in the top drawer." They were. All very neat.

Only problem--was he his own first victim
or last killer?--& which came first, the urge
to die or the itch to write the note?
                              Too easy,
in this hour of gin & bruised eyelids,
after I've filed my report . . . the notes
keep sliding in. I keep the safety off.

Regrets, *or* A Crutch for the Crab

If I had, with one and the same
sweeping grandiloquent gesture, thrown
on my cloak and rushed over to my employer's suite
to point out the cruelty of his Eat-the-Poor policies,
had I resigned then and there on principle
and then driven home by the back road,
the llamas trapped in the burning barn
would be alive today.

Or if I had only refused to testify!
Then the lynching party would not have stumbled on
the frail elderly couple
busily eviscerating the lost Swedish mountaineers.

(Many and labyrinthine are the ways
of shrugging off the world's weight.)

Alternatively, had I not lingered
over my coffee at the 10:30 break,
not cajoled Mildred at the diner
into pouring that one last cup; had I
rushed back to my desk, the overheated furnace
would not have exploded, burying
my attractive secretary Daisy
and the new kittens she had brought to work that day.

(Sempiternal and submarine the ways
of ignoring all but the middle distance
when obligatory tragedy looms.)

Most hurtfully: had I not been sole sponsor
of a Sunday School outing wherein

Sue and Brad met as teens, courted, wed,
had three lovely children, and then underwent
a bitter, mutually recriminatory divorce--
those children would not now be staring
at the trailer TV in a narcotic haze,
nor would I be thrashing myself with birches to this day.

New Poems

(1998-2001)

WAITING FOR YOU AT THE WESTERN MOTEL

(After Hopper)

Sleek clues: the hills
myopic slabs of moon, the pale blonde waiting
on the double bed, her dress somber
as dried blood but her breasts
a threat aimed dead ahead, like
your car's headlights and grill-teeth out the window.

At your entrance her face has turned,
her thumb a claw on the footboard.
"Where have you been? What kept you?"

How far will you two take each other
before one falls off the edge
of the known West?
"And which one will?"

No clouds outside, no pictures
on the walls. So many blanks
you should have filled in by now:
the nametags hanging from the luggage,
the picture frame on the bedstand, the bed
and chair, the walls, the land itself
bare as a hall of mirrors.
Still she keeps looking at you,
but you can't move
into the picture, can't alter
these expectations and alarms, can't help
breathing in this pale wash of sky,
cold sunlight slanting, getting late:
transient sun devils
one by one tying her down
to this trip, this room, tying you to her.

107

TRYST AND AFTERBURN

Dearest, we could have done without
the laughing waterfall, but never
without our strategem: meet as spies,
the aquarium at one.

You'd know me by my harpoon.
You'd open your diver's helmet
and utter the code: "Where Chinatown?"
Then I: "Is closed too late."

And then our casual exchange of airs,
of blueprints: how to build a bomb
to get us through this meeting--no,
no good, we found ourselves

useless at the prosperity
erupting everywhere around us
(the escalators, the new whale tanks),
not to mention your narcoleptic swoons.

Still, you *were* lovely, waking intermittently
and blinking behind the dolphins,
your very eyes thalassic.
All this so long ago, before

you chose to go mad, leave me
your furnishings, your taffetas.
Sorry I never sent them on
once you were settled out there

on your pillar in the desert,
but here in your old room
it keeps getting darker.
I had to throw out everything

to find a little comfort, turn
and turn, stretch out beneath
the false bottom of your trunk,
for sleep in stranded sympathy.

THE KING'S ROUTINE

I respond to your rage
with the gauzy uppercut of quiet

& a baseball stat, to which
you respond with the salt tears, typhoons &

tridents of your tidal nature, dear.
I down a bourbon in your honor.

Then it's out for some beers
with the guys, see the game, on the drive back

fuck a whore in the tunnel.
She listens to me! Comprehensively,

I'm telling her about you.
In a week or so I'm home,

but you turn away in bed,
& by morning there you are

complaining of weight & hair gain.
By night, it's weight & hair loss. I'm sorry

but cruciferous--don't you see
my name peeling from our mailbox, all

those months and years behind
on the mortgage, on your breasts,

on the treehouse for Billy? Can't you feel
what I feel--the weight of my shoes?
Why do you refuse to go the last mile in them?

SAVING THE SABER TOOTH

Souvenirs are best when stolen.
This one, fissured, priceless, you need
to keep in the attic until the finest

hush between commercials, when
you climb to it, touch it, lift it
to the hooded light. Suddenly

the weather turns black, famous;
neighbors at their windows look your way
hungering for the reward,

or would they treasure it too?
They're no better--what if
they find you alone one night

under a stroke? What if
they ransack the attic?
Then again, between their cars

and babies, they might see
the heaven they've failed
to feed. This rarest tooth,

the remains of the tiger
snowed away eons ago,
is all you have, all they want.

FARM DREAMS

With white-hot clouds I clasp you, blushing sow,
to my heart! In turn you nuzzle, murmur
pinkly in my ear, your many-nippled
endowments--neither of us dares
disturb the moment's poise. To grunt aloud,
to populate or fertilize the fields,
would be to drift among somnambulists:
a life spent grading eggs by size.

Mondays I line up alone
for my wages, and Pa always says "Boy,
the best sauce is humble pie." My farm dreams
stir again, a spread of my own, bringing home
your bacon--but to what home? None here.

When silos collide,
only the worst of weather can ensue:
see where the almanac is shredding its own
forecasts out of fear.

TODAY'S HISTORY AND HOPES

This is not the day of the plot on Hitler's life,
though nearly, nor the day the Eagle landed on the moon.
--Oh shit, the World Series is nine months away!
But okay--the diner opens at six sharp, a few stores by eight,
and there are shopping services I can access
around the clock, their voices just as cheerful as exact.

Or why not try the blooper show, the obit pages, solitaire,
the ape movies on Channel Nine,
the crossword puzzle or, on my way to the john,
quiz the family portraits hanging in the hallway,
dimming. Seems the line is dying out.

You'd think the day would be prouder
than to hang around in a haze, not quite sun
nor cloud, only a chance of a monsoon in Burma.
You'd certainly think I'd have more ambition
than to be padding invisibly
around the house. The trouble is,
I never remember meeting me unless
I pay myself compliments: call it flogging with lilacs.

And you'd think I'd have more shame
than to take credit for this, the day
Mary Baker Eddy was born, she
            "who was to break off with the spiritualist
            Phineas B. Quimby and declare
            sickness a sin in her own way: Christian Science."

Reader, the quotation marks are mine.

BUT THE HUMAN VARIETIES!

At the market, this cardboard sign: "Homeless dog and Vietnam vet--
    Please help."
The man is scowling, filthy. Far easier to give to the dog, a handsome
    collie with his own bowl for your change.

We know dogs: those large eyes lifting to us at evening in unqualified need,
        just as we know the cat's lithe stretch and arch independence
    are our tribute too: the writhing against our legs, the purr.
Animals never curse us, never make angry underground films about their
        deprived childhoods; only at our worst suffer and die avertedly.
Even a goldfish--a dime's worth of feed and it flips around the tank;
    without, it dies and floats gaping.

But the human varieties!--

For gold-diggers on the Riviera looking for their sugar-daddies, "Love
    Is a Ball."
For a slum kid turned necrophiliac, it's "A Dog From Hell."
For a lovely Eurasian doc and her daring Yank reporter, it proves
        "A Many-Splendored Thing."
And listen: for a black family from Detroit trying California, it's
        "Not Enough."
This just in: for a crusading radio announcer (played by Ronald Reagan)
    who challenges the politicos, it's "On The Air."

And right now? It's spare change and good luck, a certain wistfulness
    in the autumn breeze, tail wagging, panting to please, while
    his owner's gone off to use the McDonald's john.

HANDOUT

"All hunger is repulsive
and puts on
an ugly face."

--William Carlos Williams

Please mister, a little change
in my life.
I'm after time and space
but I'll take money if that's all you can spare.

You think this is easy for me?
I the great-grand-nephew
of the martyred leader
of the revolutionary forces of Ireland,
or possibly Israel.
Italy maybe, depending on your conception of history.

Please, just enough for an Ivy League education,
a home in Greenwich, Connecticut,
a wealthy and beautiful wife.
Then I'll gladly leave you alone
to your al fresco dining
with your lovely wife, girlfriend, daughter, whoever she is.

Believe me, I don't want to distract you
from your hors d'oeuvres and your financial speculations,
and I don't want to bore you with my problems,
my nervous twitch due to Mom's masturbation.
(She worked on the assembly line when Dad was supervisor.
They had a fling in the men's room.
Now he's the head of General Motors.
Never did acknowledge me. Never gave me a dime.

She put me up for adoption
due to my head being caved in on the side.
You can see it here, when I bow to you.)

Adopted by Sikh terrorists
I learned to hate the English and carry explosives.
At ten I escaped to the streets,
peddled my ass or anybody else's.

A cat may have it easy but not me.
A cat doesn't beg. A cat commands.
Nothing's good enough for a cat, especially yours I bet.
Well I won't go on about cats.
The pain in my back interferes with my brain.
Never been properly diagnosed.
Maybe they'll name the disease after you
if you contribute enough to my cure.

Problems like these, you'd beg too.
Naturally I take a drink now and then, a toke, why not.
And not much opportunity for personal hygiene
so I'll stay downwind of your vichyssoise.

Just a little change
for the better,
all I'm asking. Too little to notice even.
The trickle-down theory
pissed on my head. That's a joke.

I'd sing and dance but you'd regret it.
Besides, charity for nothing, pure charity
does you more credit in heaven
than cutting a deal with me.

Aren't you afraid I'll bleed on you, maybe vomit
or reach out and stain your white linen suit?
Have a seizure and fall on this orchid centerpiece?

Oh well it's enough for me
that you're weeping helplessly, spontaneously,
converting by what miracle your tears to saliva
to swallow your chocolate mousse.

Just a little change and that's it--I'm gone.
Maybe a chairmanship on your board,
but non-binding on my time.
This is after all my one vocation
and you my truest apostle.

THE BAD THIEF ON THE CROSS

In my position here
            you can no doubt understand
I don't believe in you
            nothing personal listen
in a little while
            time sure flies when you're having fun
I won't believe in me
            or anything else either

But just on the chance
            you've got special connections
prove it
            save yourself & while you're at it me too
then I'll believe
            I'll believe anything you want

& don't listen to the pious putz over there on your right
            he's the one got us caught
& now he says we deserve this
            I ask you
a little stealing just an old donkey a couple blankets
            deserves this?

& you don't have to remember me
            in your kingdom or wherever you're supposed to be going
I don't have to have a nice position
            next to you with a title & five meals a day & plenty
            of wine & a good salary & a woman whenever I want
okay I'm not refusing
            but the point right now is
get me out of here
            to anywhere else
or what good are you forever
            and ever amen

AT THE GRAND SPEECHES

On my way there
this old lady lay in the road,
her flung arm relinquishing
all daylight. At first

I took her for a sack
fallen off some truck;
her canvas housedress,
after all, and her white hair

could have been cotton anything.
But I was late so I left flares
at her head and feet
to warn all traffic.

At the grand speeches, the jokes
were falling off the cuff
into the ceremonial sweat
before the robes and gowns

ushered us into the cocktail room
where the Dean issued
a personal: *Desire seance
with martyr declared legally dead.*

The old lady--the very thought
of sacrificing her!--and I
did, broke down, too easy
a weeper, I confess, but only

a small scene, no comparison
to the grandeur of this occasion.

Door to Door

I was in the bedroom botching the haircuts
on the last of the six illegal Mexicans I'd agreed to shelter
--my good intentions for grooming them all awry--

when the doorbell sent them running to the basement.
It was the Apostles going door to door, asking
Don't you think the world's in a sorry fix?

Well, I said (the air they brought in replete
with bluejays and exhaust),
aren't we the faux-fixers after all?

That's our point, they said, a rosy pair
in matched safari apparel. Exactly!
May we come in a moment?

I could picture the Mexicans downstairs breathing
carefully, leaning on my piles of junk,
misbarbared and my clothes too large for them.

They'd had three nights of half-sleep and then
later this morning the truck would wheel them
further north, to another halfway house.

The Apostles barged in and
I gave them some cookies, then put on Chopin,
so as not to arouse suspicions.

As they asked me where I planned
to spend eternity, I saw out the window
the Mexicans ducking and running out

toward the Apostlemobile, small, but four-door.
Have another cookie? I asked,
wondering at how quickly they were able to roll it

down the road, get it started up
out of earshot, and then how all six
managed to squeeze in. Being thin helped.

The Apostles began to describe eternity
with its green pastures, though
I thought the Flight from Egypt

might have been more apropos, considering
that these illegals had parted the waters of the Rio Grande
on their wet backs--though it always closed again.

Hadn't they earned a little of this country,
its windows, dogs, barbed wire, its streets, that car?
I was inclined, though too shy, to suggest

to the Apostles my idea
of a more interactive eternity,
to interrupt them: saying, "Yes, yes, the world is fallen

but exhileratingly open--indeed,
some of us, though hopelesly lost,
are right now going for American-style record speed."

SUBSISTENCES

Right after I left
to try my hand farming
in the loam beds of passing trucks,
my little town shut down.

I go back now and then,
kick a stone off the sidewalk, stare
at my fractured face in the shop windows,
stop at the boarded-up diner

and wish for it still--
that peanut butter pie
sliding down my gullet
like a pedal-steel tune down the air

as we sat by the jukebox,
when in our way of courtship
I'd let Ingrid buy me one more slice.
In return she got to hear my theory:

how I could tell the deaf from the lame
simply by bumping them
and whispering "Ooh la-la!"
courtesy Miss Violet's French class. (That's Vee-oh-LAY.)

Now there's only Hans
left here. Huge, he shambles
around the deserted train station,
fixes splints on dead pigeons,

subsists on the stale beer
the social worker leaves out for him.
Time for a libation, he pours
a little down my shirtfront,

then he affixes a couple of splintered crossties
to our legs, in honor of the town
disappearing again
the moment I'm in my car.

Always late for recall, I pull down
some cobwebs from the corner for us--
chewy, and much more nutritious
than the long silence howling down the track.

TRAVEL'S GREATEST HITS

In Kalamazoo in those days
I kept bumping into Picasso
though honestly he was running with a different crowd.
He advised me to stick to napkin folding
which I did so definitively
the local artisans, enraged, drove me out of town.

In Muncie on the other hand
the fine dust of ages would filter down into my hair.
Very little there for an Armenian masseur to do
and although I was neither
I was reviled in the town square for doing nothing.

Yes a man was a man then in Sheboygan.

In Saginaw more of a problem
finding a bottle late at night.
After they closed the slaughterhouses
there was the music from car radios
along the bloody canal where I tried to sleep.

In Kenosha: fond memories of the axe murderer's childhood.

In Milwaukee you could see blinking
the cold lights up the hill,
the mansion where the old ladies still flew the Nazi flag
even though the mayor had asked them to desist
since this was still the Second World War
and the breakfast in frozen goatskins would hit you hard and early.

Easy to take umbrage there in Muskegon.
Easy to remember Racine's nights of love if there were any.

In those days love sang on strings of Christmas holly
or came crawling full-fanged through the swamps,
grunting and groaning and knocking over the bed-lamp.

But where are those swamp people now?

Where did they go, Elkhart's early-morning clouds like smeared eggwhites
and the freight handlers' fingers stained from cigarettes?
Where now the arguments about the best girls' team--
the Grand Rapids Chicks or the Rockford Peaches?
I fell for the gaps between the teeth
of Chicks shortstop Corky Olinger.
Short was my favorite position then as now.

Where are you, Corky?
Where is your love that was always there
to question my early despatches? To mock my typing?
Where is our love of distances, maybe to South Bend tonight?
Or waiting for me next week in Waukesha?
The love that was always my best reason to keep on traveling?

MY FAVORITE MOVIES

Running away from you, is it better to be
a singing cowboy, and you at Mass
with your beautiful Irish boys? Or better
to be falsely accused
of killing the sheriff on a sweaty night?
Or be a narcoleptic hustler nodding under the manic clouds?

Running away, but first I make sure
to tape your tape of *Mutiny on the Bounty* (1935 version)
the movie you and your husband started out with.

Or better to be a streetsweeper, hated by my twin,
who turns up, after 25 hurtful years,
fighting at my side on the Paris barricades?
Or--and no final choice, the tapes
and channels never end--to be the wife marooned
for seven years with a hairy stranger
who never washes and keeps making passes,
only to finally return home, my hair a mess,
and learn my husband has declared me legally dead
and wants to marry Marge, his secretary?

Yes to these lives and more, why not
be Charles Boyer who, on my wedding night
with bored socialite Marlene Dietrich in the Sahara,
sips a liqueur and recalls--My God,
I'm a lapsed Trappist monk and must repent!

Here in your living room's half-light, the audience
is ghostly but more real, especially
those kids groping in the back row
up behind the sofa. Or, if you come back

to find me, bags packed, and try
to "acknowledge" me, I might as well
be the blind mother of a family of crazed epileptics,
all of them trying to kill me for my wealth.

LEAVING LABRADOR

Showed up to the funeral right at ten.
Seems I got the day wrong,

nobody there but the mermaid,
said Better *not* be Friday, I fish on Friday.

Here I'd got all dressed up, suit and tie,
and nothing doing but fat families in shorts

hauling free of each other
to get to their favorite stores in the mall.

An extra day, but when you're retired,
three children gone bad, you learn

or you don't, you cover the grease spot
on the rug with another rug,

just smaller, make sure one corner points
to the sofa and one to the chair, arty like that.

Like yesterday--couldn't find the food
to please my cat Harold. Hasn't been back since.

Nothing on TV? You can read how
they're still leaving Labrador, but less

than last year, and Adora Freake has been crowned
Miss Teen Lube Job after she won

the baton-twirling competition
at the Arts and Culture Center in Bayonne.

Judging by her picture, all those greased ringlets,
why would her baton, once she'd set it twirling

up in the lights, soaring over Portugal,
not want to come down? Adora now,

you'd be worth missing any funeral for, right
on time. Besides which, I didn't know the deceased.

KILLER'S NEWS

Not every killer is suitable news.
Not every hero comes home. Don't bother me,
I'm trying to concentrate

on the latest escapee
from Death Row, seems he cultivated lilacs
in his cell, kept pictures of Jesus
and remembered the birthdays of all the reporters
who interviewed him, brought him chocolates.

My hobby? Forgetting this room
every ten minutes for the news.

What would I have done
younger, stronger, in his place?
Studied semiotics with the junkie down the hall?

Or would I have picked up my gun
and walked up onto the first back porch, easy,
the family sitting down to Sunday lunch
and for an instant looking at me pleasantly,
expecting I might be somebody
welcome, somebody bringing news?

ANONYMOUS URGES

I didn't know you were dead. I was just leaving
the factory. There by the gate
your dirty raincoat flapped and waved.

I'd memorized the way
to your door, figured miles per gallon,
shortest routes, the time saved
had I made it. But always
the problem--how could I be
the one left behind?

I know I'd promised to help you age,
but sometime you must have decided:
why wait? And no expert
ever around when you need one.

Then I'd meant to get there
before your remains did, cushion the blow
for your plants and the cat.
I'd meant to enshroud your pictures
and dirty dishes, sell the house, or
no--burn everything, nothing
ever clean as ashes on my tongue.

WHY I LIVE AT THE ARMORY

In the tall dim armory on Lex
and 25th I take up residence.
All the greatcoated regiments
faded to photos on the walls
look down over their moustaches,
find me civilian, lax.

The Great Hall has seen balls,
receptions, the fans and lashes
of the inviting belles.
Still, I have my teatime
and my close-order drills
best practised all alone,

my bunk that tastes of ashes
and my shit-on-a-shingle--
good old army swill
I cook myself, following
instructions for six hundred.
The rest I freeze. Time tells

of my brother in ROTC
at the commisioning ceremony,
dignitaries assembling.
He fired and missed the bullseye,
the target, the wall behind.
The bullet ricocheted

and everybody ducked
--quick!--down on the ground.
The major swore, wondered
who'd given him the rifle.

Now I sweep up, bedecked
with medals from a raffle.

Here at my desk, I'm
writing to the widows
of Antietam and Bellow Wood:
"In heaven there are windows
where they peer out for good,
your husbands. Sincerely, I remain . . . ."

Only a Local Call Away

There's an old dead man lying by my door
in a baby basket. Timing is nothing,
it seems, to some people. Only last week
a radiant girl knocked: white gown, white wings.
Samples rich and rare, she said,
for the man of the house. None here? And she had
the decency to leave. But here is a case
too misbegotten to solve, I'm late for work
and the head and limbs sprawling out,
a question of the time it takes
my causes to register: chain myself
to him? And then what to tell the police?

An issue of common hygiene! I'm ready
to leave, all carefully packed:
my plastic animals, comforter,
Expert's Guide to Experts. All due speed
but no haste, not after all
these years, these rooms
not fit to die in,
too all-consuming for anyone to clean.

What Really Happens

happens hushed as my forgetting
to rescue the deaf bride
from her shipwreck in the ice
those centuries ago;

happens late, in the corner
of the museum, where
the mice feed; what reporter
could be bothered?

Ever less relevant,
a mental patient sits
away from the light,
staring at radiator waves,

serpents cherishing their dust.
Outside, pagodas of snow
baffle the traffic
in its one vow: vengeance.

When the zeros click
to twelve, and she
in her veil arrives late,
sweating not with my stay

of execution, but rather
the warden's pizza order,
then this was never my life
under another, higher name.

In Love Solving the Bowery Murders

In love with you at fifteen is best
here in my storefront office on the Bowery
solving murders through careful forensic investigation.

The sun streams in blackly on the dustballs,
on the general filth standing up all around.
It coats the radiators, pipes, everything
though I keep my desk clean
and am busy comparing the fingerprints and knuckle hairs
on the bodies they keep wheeling in on hand trucks
and stacking up. I'm getting way behind.

Then you come in. You sit on my lap.
Pink sweater, little white tennis skirt.
Kiss kiss, copious kisses.

When I come up for air I see
our friend Steve walking on the red light at Bleecker.
He's hit by a nun's car.

She asks his name and says I'm Sister Cathy. Hi.
Really sorry, Steve. She drives off.
Leaves him cursing her screaming, My leg is broken!

I can't blame her. She's probably late
for her hospital visits to the poor and then
she'll have to swat her fifth grade students.
Remember this is back when I was fifteen.
And now I get busy kissing you some more.

Steve comes crawling in still cursing her
and I ask him did he get her license number.
But he won't stop cursing and suddenly he dies.
So it's murder after all, another case to solve.

And now you go off to your tennis lesson
in your pert little pleated skirt, swish swish out the door.
But the bodies keep piling up higher and soon they'll start stinking
and I can't use formaldehyde until I've examined each one.

If I fail to determine all these causes of death
will I keep my job?
I like this Bowery sunshine
and where else but in this dream would you visit me?
We're middle-aged now and married to others
if I were to wake up.

So it's back to the microscope and slides and all my notes.
Somebody brings in a photo of Sister Cathy
and somebody else phones in her convent's address
so now we're getting somewhere.

You come back saying you've missed me.
Somebody stole the tennis net
so instead you went out for coffee and bought this bridal veil
off a street lady and now you lean over and kiss me.

And now you tell me you're in love
with the marital/martial arts sign you saw on the street just now.
We talk of honeymoons we could spend in tall rooms.
We talk of drinking in cabarets.
What do we know about cabarets? We're fifteen. We're only guessing
but we know tall rooms are best
for tall thoughts reaching into some anonymous future.

Looking into your eyes I see how life is going to save us
from having to answer eagerly and eternally
the world's indiscriminate offers.
Are they bargains?
We only wish.

NOTE TO ELLYSUE

Another grim upstate April, and no
one context will cheer me except
the school of philosophy you founded
and still lead: Exasperationism.
And your major works ("They Got
a Lotta Nerve," "Where Do You
Get Off," and "You Guys All Think
You're Princes") as articulated
daily by you in Brooklyn
will serve me right until
the sun comes out, and
real summer, all ten months
of it, with mosquitos.

Til then, keeping busy is the key
to keeping busy. Hope this note
finds you well, well along whatever way
loses us all inside itself.

ELDER HOSTEL

What did I come in here for?
Shafts of whitewashed light
burrow the dark deeper
into my swaying head.

The right tool is somewhere
in the room I left. Outside,
a woodpecker has started his tattoo:
somebody being drummed out
of the regiment, in the old westerns.

Here are some shirts
I haven't worn in years,
and a dim negative--
the cabin where our younger selves
bled inside out, her hair and my beard
prophetically shock-white.

Here is a hand of aces and eights;
which one do I lead?
A spider tickles the hair
on the back of my head; he knows
what he came in here for.

Outside, others make the noises
of knowing too: their tires' screams
are falling on me, whose walls
wave deeper out of reach.

YOUR AD IN THIS SPACE

This morning dreaming of your love
as Vespucci dreamed of America
and he the first to see what it could mean--
"My own name on a hemisphere--Look!
World's Biggest Billboard!"

Hiding out from your love on the road,
our local team losing, trouble finding the ball.
Plenty of sky out there,
but never enough detail to read into.
Your Russian-seductive eyelashes would have helped.

This morning your love sent a man with a gun
walking through my doorway: "You know why I'm here."
But no, I haven't been following the plot;
I got up late. No codes, no data to fill the blanks,
no secret punches other than your love.

MERCY OF MARRIAGE

You never take me anywhere.
Rather than see you get off with a light divorce,
I'll kill us both. Who were you planning to elope with
there in the den where the TV took my youth?

Done! Or almost--in my case, a flesh wound,
irksome. Alone together alone,
in the shade of my long sentence,
I reach out to kiss you, but your lovely hair
is stone-engraved. Now I must make do
with memories of us, eroding from the start.
Nor is this shade what it used to be, as the sun sags.

On his Tuesdays off, our marriage counselor
comes by to visit me, begging for mercy.

Acknowledgements

Poems in Collections:
Audit Press: *Landscape of Skin and Single Rooms*
Monday Morning Press: *Fat Chances*
Stream Books: *Celebrations*
Linear Arts Books: *Come Back Vanishing*
Rattapallax Press: *Saving the Saber Tooth*

Individual Poems:
The Brooklyn Review: "Alonzo's Crib Death," "Women," "Travel's
  Greatest Hits," "What Really Happens;"
The Carleton Miscellany: "What Happens to Fathers and Children;"
Chester H. Jones Contest Winner: "The Discreet Guest;"
Concerning Poetry: "Where You Were Last Seen," "Winter's Room;"
Encore: "Letting the Pine Tree Keep Track;"
Granite: "The Smile of a Confident Man;"
Grasslands Review: "Some Alternatives to the Crash That Killed
  Sigrid;"
Gulfstream: "Tonight the Widows Are Sailing;"
The Helen Review: "Obligations Towards My Shoes;"
The Little Review: "A Hope for My Child, Not Yet Born," "How to
  Ward off Burglars," "Your Abandoned Child, New Jersey;"
Mainline: "The Right Conditions;"
The Manhattan Review: "The Barber Shop of The Dead," "Who Fell
  Away First?";
Medicinal Purposes Literary Review: "Mail Order," "Elder Hostel,"
  "Note to EllySue;"
Mind the Gap: "Farm Dreams;"
Monday Morning Wash: "A Flourishing Mother at Rush Hour;"
New York Quarterly: "Marriage;"
Onset Review: "Mistakes of Waking Urban," "You Can Too;"

On the Bus/Rattle: "Long Dark Entanglements;"
The Paris Review: "The Addicts," "The Recollection-Hole," "The
   Visiting Distinguished, *or* Do Your Own Weeping;"
Poetry Australia: "The Whine of the Red Shoes;"
Poetry Motel: "Old Miser;"
Prairie Schooner: "Daddy Bad-News," "Earning a Name," "Who
   Can Say What the Dead Miss Most?";
Quarter Horse: "When You Die in New York," "For the New
   Year;"
Rattapallax: "Doom & Me," "Regrets, *or* A Crutch for the Crab,"
   "Tryst and Afterburn;"
Salonika: "The Ferryman and I;"
Shantih: "The Dilating Theater;"
Skylark: " Retiree;"
The Smith: "Afternoon in a Far Town;"
Southern Poetry Review: "Ask Me In;"
Stand: "I Have To Live;"
Tamarind Review: "Romance Language Lesson," "Do-Si-Do," "Do
   You Have This Disease?";
The Windless Orchard: "Accidents on the Highway," "Ashamed of
   Any Fires," "Dancing Our Family Dead," "The Hiding Wife,"
   "The Lady of the Wastes;"
Wisconsin Review: "Calling Home From Nowhere," "Getting Back
   At."

CD LISTING